THE JOY OF Duets

ISBN 978-0-634-06674-0

HAL•LEONARD®
CORPORATION
7777 W. BLUEMOUND RD. P.O. BOX 13819 MILWAUKEE, WI 53213

Visit Hal Leonard Online at
www.halleonard.com

CONTENTS

ANGEL

SECONDO

Words and Music by
SARAH McLACHLAN

Moderately, with feeling

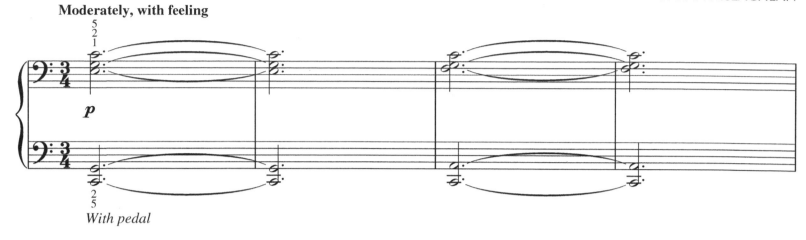

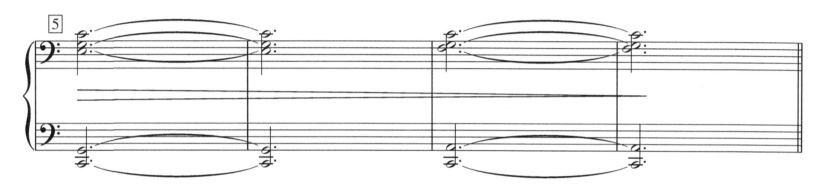

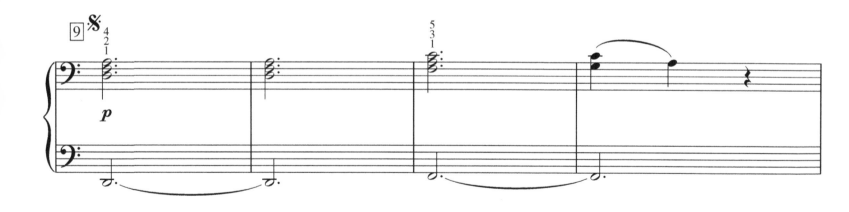

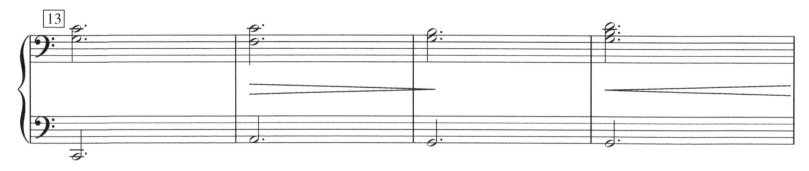

ANGEL

PRIMO

Words and Music by
SARAH McLACHLAN

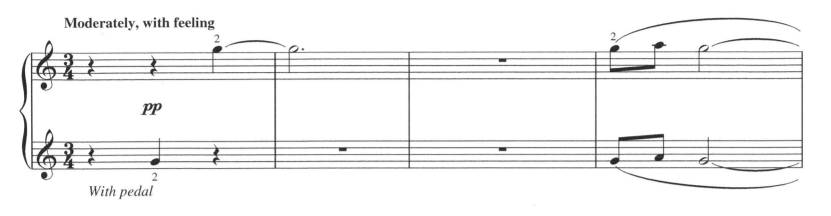

SECONDO

PRIMO

SECONDO

PRIMO

SECONDO

PRIMO

SECONDO

PRIMO

DON'T KNOW WHY

SECONDO

Words and Music by
JESSE HARRIS

Moderately slow

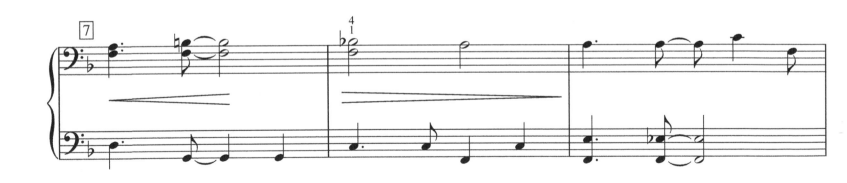

DON'T KNOW WHY

PRIMO

Words and Music by
JESSE HARRIS

Moderately slow

SECONDO

PRIMO

SECONDO

PRIMO

(EVERYTHING I DO)
I DO IT FOR YOU
from the Motion Picture ROBIN HOOD: PRINCE OF THIEVES

SECONDO

Words and Music by BRYAN ADAMS,
ROBERT JOHN LANGE and MICHAEL KAMEN

(EVERYTHING I DO)
I DO IT FOR YOU

from the Motion Picture ROBIN HOOD: PRINCE OF THIEVES

PRIMO

Words and Music by BRYAN ADAMS,
ROBERT JOHN LANGE and MICHAEL KAMEN

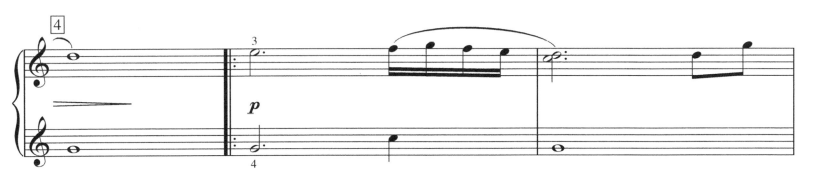

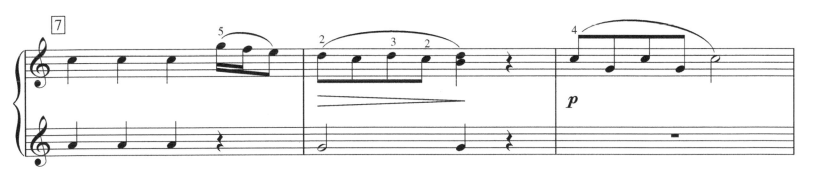

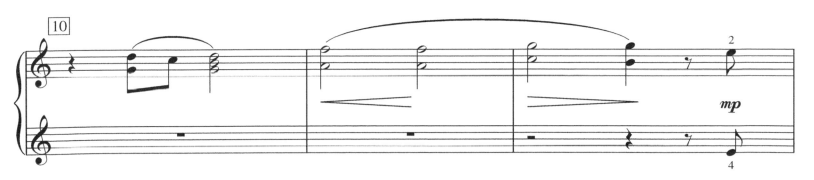

SECONDO

PRIMO

SECONDO

PRIMO

HARD TO SAY I'M SORRY

SECONDO

Words and Music by PETER CETERA
and DAVID FOSTER

Moderately, with expression

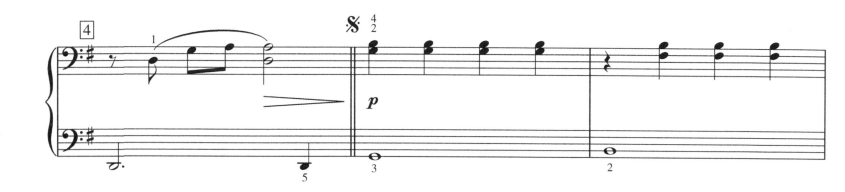

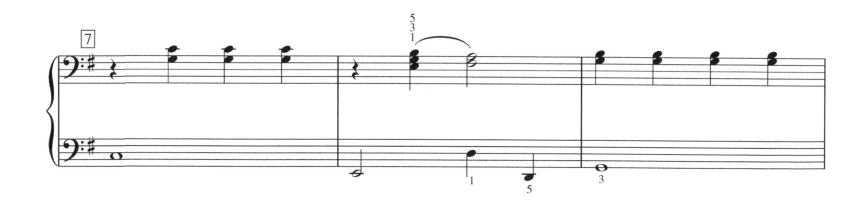

HARD TO SAY I'M SORRY

PRIMO

Words and Music by PETER CETERA
and DAVID FOSTER

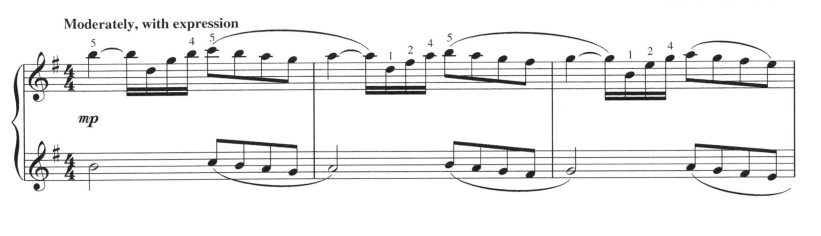

PRIMO

SECONDO

PRIMO

I GET AROUND

SECONDO

Words and Music by BRIAN WILSON
and MIKE LOVE

Bright Rock beat

I GET AROUND

PRIMO

Words and Music by BRIAN WILSON
and MIKE LOVE

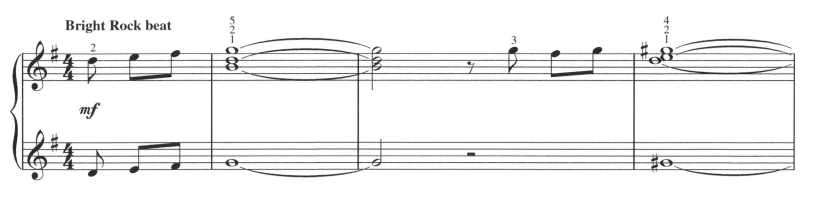

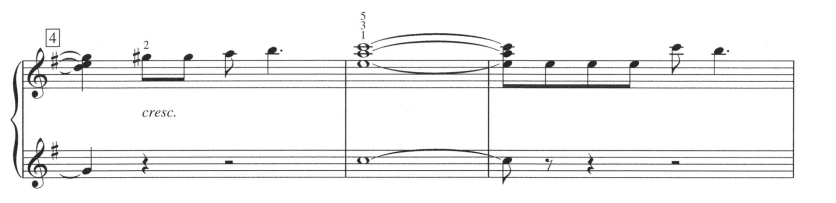

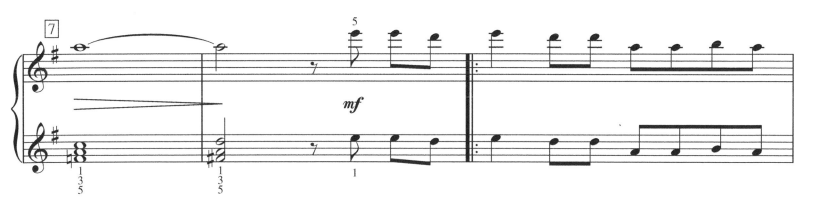

SECONDO

PRIMO

SECONDO

JUST THE WAY YOU ARE

SECONDO

Words and Music by
BILLY JOEL

Moderately

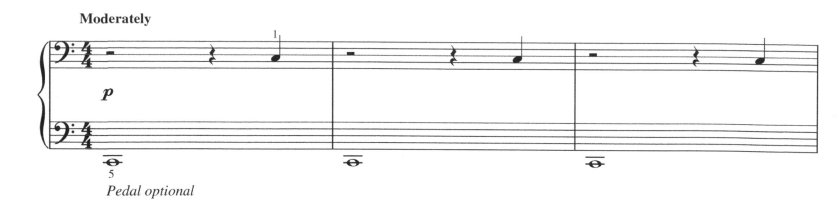

Pedal optional

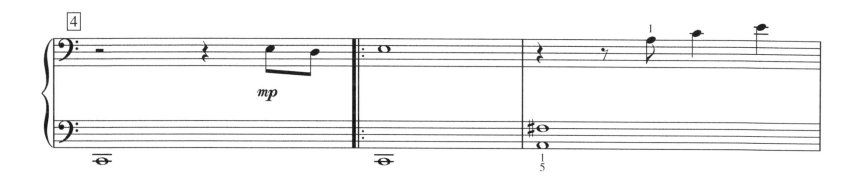

JUST THE WAY YOU ARE

PRIMO

Words and Music by
BILLY JOEL

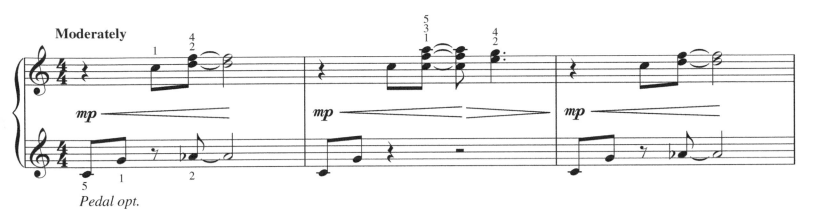

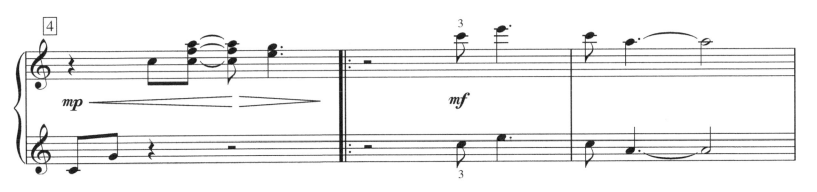

SECONDO

PRIMO

SECONDO

PRIMO

SECONDO

PRIMO

SECONDO

PRIMO

LET IT BE

SECONDO

Words and Music by JOHN LENNON
and PAUL McCARTNEY

LET IT BE

PRIMO

Words and Music by JOHN LENNON
and PAUL McCARTNEY

SECONDO

LINUS AND LUCY

SECONDO

By VINCE GUARALDI

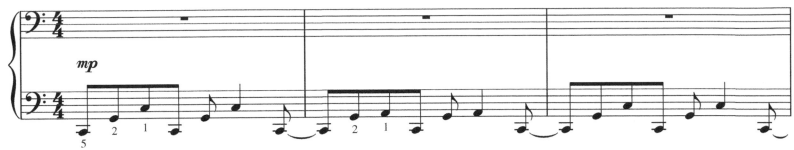

LINUS AND LUCY

PRIMO

By VINCE GUARALDI

Moderately

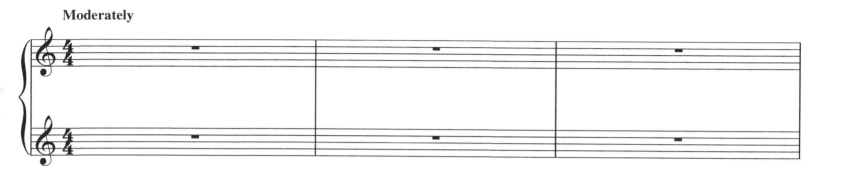

SECONDO

PRIMO

SECONDO

PRIMO

SECONDO

PRIMO

SECONDO

D.S. al Coda

PRIMO

MY HEART WILL GO ON

(Love Theme from 'Titanic')

from the Paramount and Twentieth Century Fox Motion Picture TITANIC

SECONDO

Music by JAMES HORNER
Lyric by WILL JENNINGS

MY HEART WILL GO ON
(Love Theme from 'Titanic')
from the Paramount and Twentieth Century Fox Motion Picture TITANIC

PRIMO

Music by JAMES HORNER
Lyric by WILL JENNINGS

SECONDO

PRIMO

SECONDO

SECONDO

PRIMO

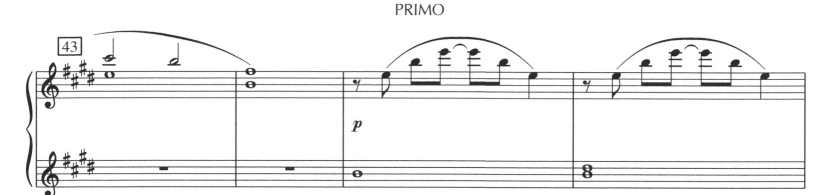

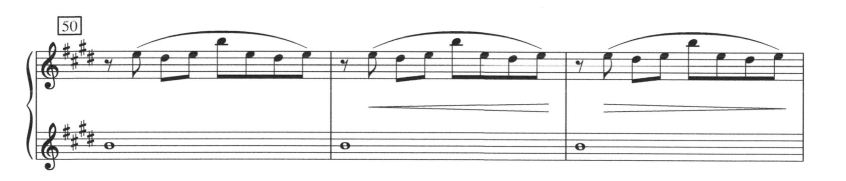

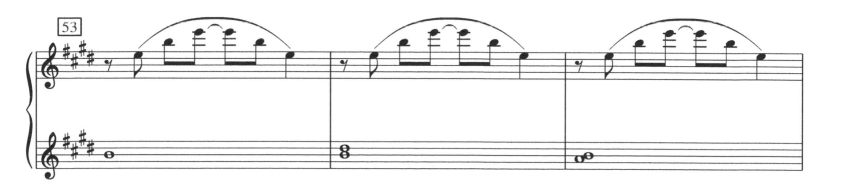

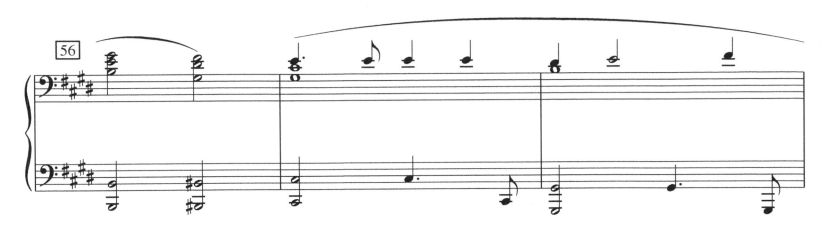

D.S. al Coda

CODA

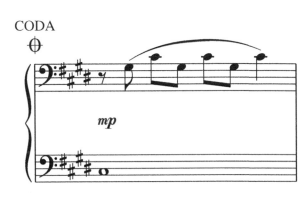

mp

cresc.

PRIMO

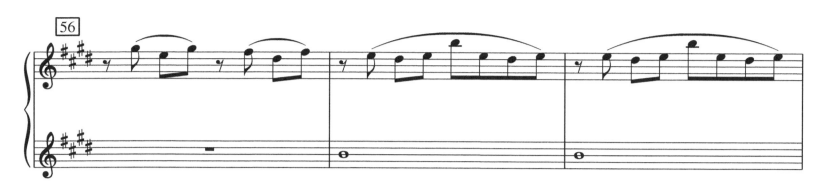

D.S. al Coda   CODA

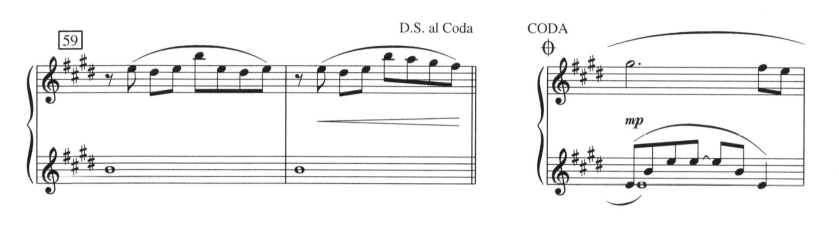

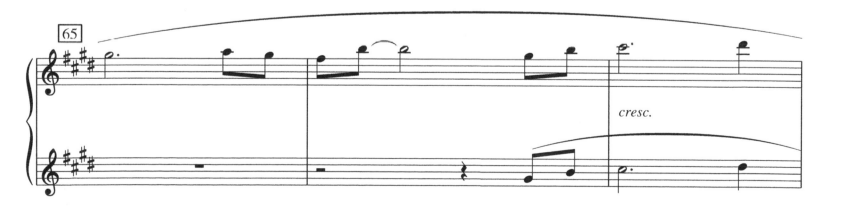

SECONDO

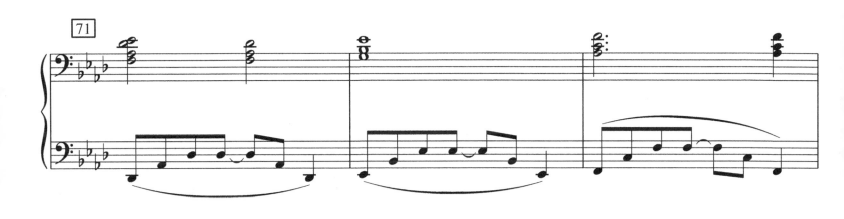

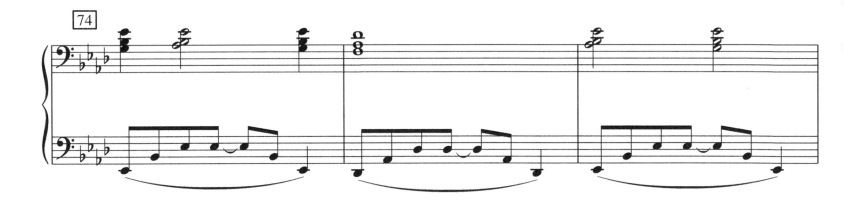

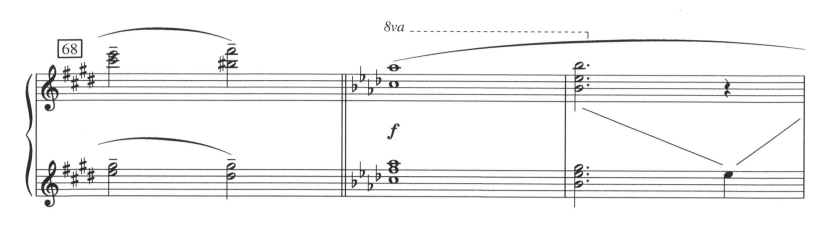

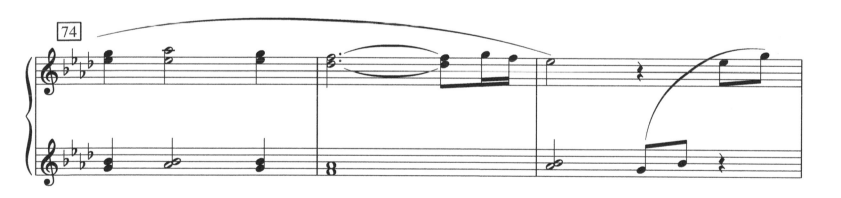

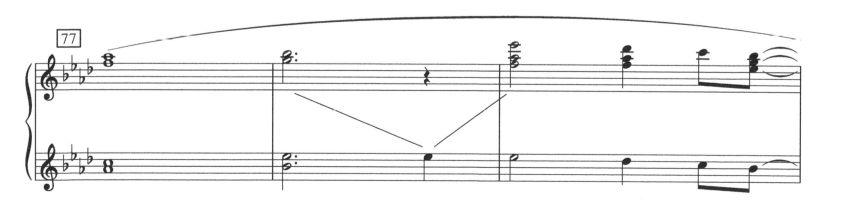

SECONDO

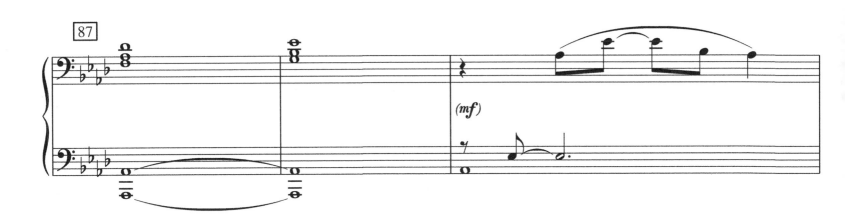

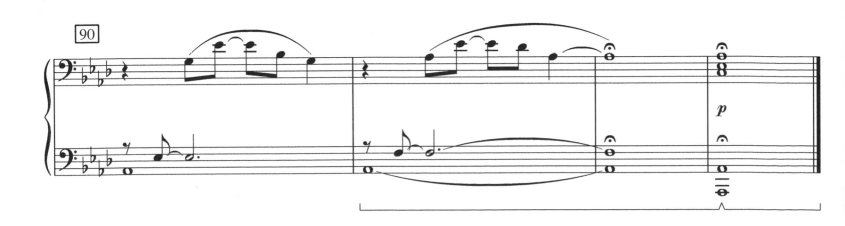

PRIMO

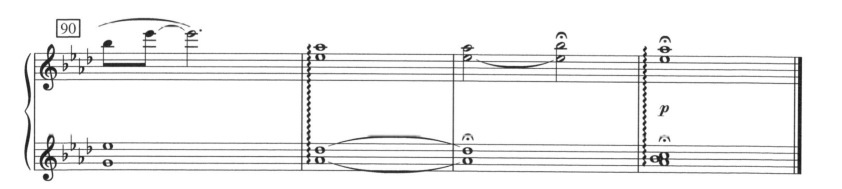

TWO WORLDS

from Walt Disney Pictures' TARZAN™

SECONDO

Words and Music by
PHIL COLLINS

TWO WORLDS
from Walt Disney Pictures' TARZAN™

PRIMO

Words and Music by
PHIL COLLINS

Piano For Two

A Variety of Piano Duets from Hal Leonard

LI – THE BEATLES PIANO DUETS – 2ND EDITION

Features 8 arrangements: Can't Buy Me Love • Eleanor Rigby • Hey Jude • Let It Be • Penny Lane • Something • When I'm Sixty-Four • Yesterday.

00290496 ....$10.95

I – BROADWAY DUETS

9 duet arrangements of Broadway favorites, including: Cabaret • Comedy Tonight • Ol' Man River • One • and more.

00292077 ....$12.99

LI – BROADWAY FAVORITES

A show-stopping collection of 8 songs arranged as piano duets. Includes: I Dreamed a Dream • If Ever I Would Leave You • Memory • People.

00290185 ....$9.95

LI – COLLECTED SACRED CLASSICS

Arranged by Bill Boyd
8 classics for piano duet, including: Ave Maria • A Mighty Fortress • Hallelujah from *Messiah* • and more.

00221009 ....$9.95

I – DISNEY DUETS

8 songs: Candle on the Water • Colors of the Wind • Cruella de Vil • Hakuna Matata • Someday • A Spoonful of Sugar • Winnie the Pooh • Zip-A-Dee-Doo-Dah.

00290484 ....$12.95

LI – DISNEY MOVIE HITS FOR TWO

9 fun favorites, including: Be Our Guest • Circle of Life • Friend like Me • Under the Sea • A Whole New World • and more.

00292076 ....$14.95

LI – DUET CLASSICS FOR PIANO

8 classical melodies, arranged as piano duets. Includes: Liebestraum (Liszt) • Minuet In G (Beethoven) • Sleeping Beauty Waltz (Tchaikovsky) • and more.

00290172 ....$6.95

LI – GERSHWIN PIANO DUETS

These duet arrangements of 10 Gershwin classics such as "I Got Plenty of Nuttin'," "Summertime," "It Ain't Necessarily So," and "Love Walked In" sound as full and satisfying as the orchestral originals.

00312603 ....$10.95

I – GREAT MOVIE THEMES

8 movie hits, including: Chariots of Fire • Colors of the Wind • The Entertainer • *Forrest Gump – Main Title* • Theme from *Jurassic Park* • Somewhere in Time • Somewhere, My Love • *Star Trek® – The Motion Picture* • and more.

00290494 ....$9.95

UI – LOVE DUETS

7 songs: All I Ask of You • Can You Feel the Love Tonight • Can't Help Falling in Love • Here, There, and Everywhere • Unchained Melody • When I Fall in Love • A Whole New World (Aladdin's Theme).

00290485 ....$8.95

LI – ANDREW LLOYD WEBBER PIANO DUETS

arr. Ann Collins
8 easy piano duets, featuring some of Andrew Lloyd Webber's biggest hits such as: All I Ask of You • Don't Cry for Me Argentina • Memory • I Don't Know How to Love Him.

00290332 ....$12.95

I – MOVIE DUETS

9 songs, including: Chariots of Fire • *The Godfather* (Love Theme) • *Romeo and Juliet* (Love Theme) • Theme from *Schindler's List* • and more.

00292078 ....$9.95

UI – COLE PORTER PIANO DUETS

What a better way to play these 6 Cole Porter love songs such as "Do I Love You?" "I Love Paris," "In The Still of the Night," than with a partner?

00312680............................$9.95

UI – ROCK 'N' ROLL – PIANO DUETS

Ten early rock classics, including: Blue Suede Shoes • Don't Be Cruel • Rock Around the Clock • Shake, Rattle and Roll.

00290171............................$9.95

I – THE SOUND OF MUSIC

9 songs, including: Do-Re-Mi • Edelweiss • My Favorite Things • The Sound of Music • and more.

00290389.........................$12.95

GRADING
LI = Lower Intermediate
I = Intermediate
UI = Upper Intermediate

For More Information, See Your Local Music Dealer, or Write To:

HAL•LEONARD® CORPORATION
7777 W. Bluemound Rd. P.O. Box 13819 Milwaukee, WI 53213

www.halleonard.com